# CHI KUNG

## Increase Your Energy, Improve Your Health

Wei Yue Sun, M.D.
& Xiao Jing Li, M.D.

Sterling Publishing Co., Inc.
New York

# *Acknowledgments*

We'd like to thank the many people who helped us with this book, particularly Mr. Andrew Greenspan for his work on the photographs. Their contribution made the book possible.

**Library of Congress Cataloging-in-Publication Data**

Sun, Wei Yue
    Chi Kung : increase your energy, improve your health / by Wei Yue Sun & Xiao Jing Li.
        p.   cm.
    Includes index.
    ISBN 0-8069-9729-X
    1. Ch'i kung.  I. Li, Xiao Jing.  II. Title.
RA781.8.S83   1997
613.7´1—dc21                                                97-15299
                                                                  CIP

1  3  5  7  9  10  8  6  4  2

Published by Sterling Publishing Company, Inc.
387 Park Avenue South, New York, N.Y. 10016
© 1997 by Wei Yue Sun and Xiao Jing Li
Distributed in Canada by Sterling Publishing
c/o Canadian Manda Group, One Atlantic Avenue, Suite 105
Toronto, Ontario, Canada M6K 3E7
Distributed in Great Britain and Europe by Cassell PLC
Wellington House, 125 Strand, London WC2R 0BB, England
Distributed in Australia by Capricorn Link (Australia) Pty Ltd.
P.O. Box 6651, Baulkham Hills, Business Centre, NSW 2153, Australia
*Manufactured in the United States of America*
*All rights reserved*

Sterling  ISBN 0-8069-9729-X

# CONTENTS

# WHAT IS CHI KUNG?

Chi Kung is an art for both the body and the mind. It has been practiced for more than two thousand years in China and was created by its people to help prevent and cure diseases, protect and strengthen health, and prolong life. Although there are many different forms of Chi Kung practiced in China today, the basic components are the same: concentration, relaxation, mind exercises, breathing exercises, posture, and movement. The combination of all these parts is the key for practicing Chi Kung.

The forms of Chi Kung described in this book are the most popular ones practiced by thousands of people in China today. They are easy to learn, can obtain Chi quickly and easily, and serve as the basic foundation for the other advanced forms of Chi Kung.

Traditional Chinese medicine and modern Western medicine have already found that Chi Kung practice can modify a human body's functions in a dual aspect, such as reducing hyperactivity function while increasing deficiency function. It also can be used as a way for reducing stress and improving health. Chi Kung is one of the gems in the treasure chest of Chinese cultural heritage as well as an important part of traditional Chinese medicine.

## HISTORY

Chi Kung, as a form of exercise, has a history of several thousand years and diverse schools. In ancient times it had various names, such as XingChi (Promoting and Conducting Chi), FuChi (Taking in Chi), Tuna (Expiration Chi), AnChi (Massage), and WoKung (Lying Exercises).

The origin of Chi Kung can be traced to around 2357–2256 B.C., when the Yao people realized that dancing could strengthen a person's health. *Lu's Spring and Autumn Annals* explained that Yin had a tendency to stagnate, incubate latently, and accumulate in the body. This would cause the blocking up of water passages in the body, which prevented water from flowing to its original right passages. Chi would then stagnate in the body, and the muscles and bones would cower and shorten and could not be extended properly. Dancing was therefore created to remove any stagnation and obstruction. Some of the dances gradually developed into physical and breathing exercises that were the early stages of Chi Kung.

Certain actions, breathing, and sounds were discovered to have regulating effects on certain functions of the human body. For example, extending the limbs could dissipate heat, huddling up the body could keep out the cold, making the sound "Ha" could also dissipate heat and remove stagnancy, making the sound "Hei" could suppress and release physical strength, making the sound "Xu" could alleviate pain, etc. Lao Tzu (6th century B.C. philosopher) recorded the methods of "blowing (Chi)" and "puffing (Chi)." Chuang Tzu (6th century B.C. philosopher) further mentioned that blowing and puffing, exhaling and inhaling, getting rid of the stale and taking in the fresh, contracting like the bear and stretching like the bird all helped to prolong life.

*Jade Pendant Inscription on Chi Kung*, a historical relic of the early Spring and Autumn and Warring States periods (770 B.C.–221 B.C.), recorded the training method and theory of Chi Kung. The inscription, made up of forty-five Chinese characters engraved on a twelve-sided cylinder, stated the health-preserving principles of Chi Kung as well as the steps of transforming essence to energy to spirit: "In promoting and conducting Chi, depth promises storage, storage promises extension, extension promises descent, descent promises stability, stability promises solidness, solidness promises germination, germination promises growth, growth promises retreat, retreat leads to heaven. Heavenly Chi functions from above, earthly Chi functions from below. Conformity to this leads to life while adverseness to this leads to death."

Among the historical relics unearthed from the Han Tomb at Mawangdui, Changsha in the Hunan Province of China was a silk painting of "Daoyin illustrations" from the early Western Han Dynasty period (202 B.C.–220 A.D.). The forty-four colored Daoyin (an often used synonym for Chi Kung) illustrations show training exercises for inducing, promoting, and conducting Chi. In the Han Dynasty (202 B.C.–220 A.D.), *The Yellow Emperor's Classic of Internal Medicine*, the earliest extant general-medical collection in China, expanded Chi Kung's principles, training methods, and effects. Zhang Zhougjing, a physician of the dynasty, documented the use of Chi Kung in treating diseases. His contemporary, renowned physician Hua Tuo developed a set of exercises called "The Five-Animal Play," which mimicked the movements and gestures of the tiger, deer, bear, monkey, and bird to better circulate blood and prevent diseases.

Other records on Chi Kung are also found in *General Treatise on the Etiology and Symptomatology of Diseases* (610 A.D.) by Chao Yuanfang in the Sui Dynasty, *Prescriptions Worth a Thousand Gold for Emergencies* by the renowned physician Sun Simiao (581–682 A.D.), and *The Medical Secrets of an Official* by Wang Tao (702–772 A.D.) during the Tang Dynasty.

In modern times, a Chi Kung sanatorium was founded in 1955 in the city of Tangshan in Hebei Province to study the clinical curative effects of Chi Kung therapy. In July 1957, the Shanghai Municipal Chi Kung Sanatorium was founded. In October 1959, the Ministry of Public Health of the People's Republic of China held the First National Meeting to Exchange Experience in Chi Kung in Beidaihe in Hebei Province. Since 1978, scientific research in Beijing and Shanghai have adopted modern technology to carry out comprehensive research into Chi Kung. In recent years, Chi Kung has been widely used to treat many chronic diseases, such as chronic hepatitis, hypertension, bronchial asthma, and neurasthenia. It also has certain curative effects on some acute diseases like acute appendicitis and can serve as an anaesthesia in certain surgical operations.

The application and research of Chi Kung have also gone beyond the scope of medicine. It has been found to have a relatively high use in agriculture, military affairs, physical culture, and education. Chi Kung may play an important role in probing the secrets of the human body and life and, perhaps, in founding a new science.

## THEORY

Chi Kung is designed to train and direct your Chi (your internal energy flow) through physical and mental exercises. You associate your mind with certain posture and breathing movements to act upon your entire body. By doing this, you regulate the functional activities of the body and maintain a dynamic equilibrium. In addition, you enable your body to produce and store energy (by reducing energy consumption and increasing energy accumulation), produce the effects that regulate Yin and Yang, and emit Chi from the meridians of the body.

The term Chi Kung means "to work with Chi." According to Chinese thought, Chi is the fundamental but immeasurable substance that constitutes the universe. It exists within our body as well as throughout the natural world. In other words, Chi affects every human being both internally and externally. It can be viewed as an energy, though it cannot be measured, and all phenomena are produced by the changes and movements of Chi. In traditional Chinese philosophy and medical theories "Chi is the root of the human body; the stem and leaves would dry up without a root." Human beings connect and interact with the world through exercising their

Chi and regulating Yin and Yang. Otherwise, our bodies would tire and inevitably be unable to move.

Chi Kung is based on the theory of Yin and Yang, which is a philosophy as well as an important part of the basic theories of traditional Chinese medicine. Yin and Yang indicate the passive (Yin) and active (Yang) principles of the universe. They are opposite but complementary components that also interact with our body as well as between our body and the natural world. Their symbols are water and fire, respectively.

Yin and Yang are the law of the natural world, the great framework of everything, the parent of change, the root and beginning of life and death. All natural phenomena contain the interaction of these two poles. Nothing is ever only Yin or only Yang. In traditional Chinese medicine, balancing Yin and Yang is important to maintaining your health. The loss of their balance will cause illness or, if the imbalance remains for a long time, even death.

In Chi Kung, outward motion, relaxation, breathing, and concentration help to keep this balance. For instance, exhalation is Yang while inhalation is Yin. When you exhale, you open Yang and emit Chi. When you inhale, you close Yin and bring in Chi. If you have too much Yang, or fire, you should concentrate on exhalation. If you are deficient in Yang, you should concentrate on inhalation.

## CHI KUNG AND THE BODY

In traditional Chinese medicine, the human body has twelve physiological systems that are each associated with an internal (visceral) organ and meridian. Meridians are pathways that run throughout the body to make up an invisible network in which Chi flows. They were discovered over many centuries by acupuncturists who were looking for acupuncture points, or acupoints, and found that these points lined up to form paths throughout the body. Acupuncturists determine along which acupoint

to apply their needles, because they believe that certain illnesses are a result of Chi being blocked along the relevant meridian.

Meridian paths are categorized into twelve main meridians, fifteen collaterals, and eight extraordinary channels. Collaterals and channels are like the branches of the meridians. These meridian paths integrate all of the body's energies and relate the various organs with their functions (e.g., the meridian of the stomach influences digestion, etc.).

The visceral organs that are associated with the twelve main meridians are known as the "Five-Zang and Six-Fu Organs." They consist of the liver, heart, spleen, lungs, kidneys, stomach, small intestine, large intestine, bladder, gallbladder, and triple warmer (the thoracic, abdominal, and pelvic cavities). The pericardium was later added, presumably to provide symmetry to the system.

How some of these organs are viewed differs somewhat from modern Western medicine. Chi Kung exercises focus on the different parts of the body to stimulate the circulation of Chi in those areas. For instance, based on the Five-Zang and Six-Fu Organs theory, the heart governs mental activities, which include the spirit, consciousness, and thought—functions that are associated more with the brain. When the heart is ill, some of the symptoms can be the inability to concentrate, forgetfulness, insomnia, etc. In Chi Kung, you try to set your mind into a tranquil state so as to achieve the regulating of these "mental activities."

The heart also governs blood circulation, and its manifestation is in the face. Chi Kung exercise can also affect the Chi of the heart, which pushes the blood through the blood vessels. The result is in an even, gentle, yet forceful pulse and a ruddy and lustrous complexion.

The lungs govern Chi. Breathing exercises bring in the essential Chi from the heaven and earth and exhale the turbid Chi from our body. The lungs send the Chi down into our body and the kidneys receive it. When you bring the inhaled Chi to your *Dantian* (the center of your body, which is 2 or 3 inches below your navel; see p. 13), you achieve a state of deep, long, gentle respiration and almost imperceptible nasal breathing. This "stillness" directs the inhaled Chi from the heaven and earth to meet and combine with the Chi of the kidneys, and transform it into the Chi of the human body, enabling the internal Chi and body to strengthen rapidly.

Xu Lingtai, a famous Chinese physician (1882–1960), believed that the kidneys are "the gates of life" since they are connected to the Dantian and are in charge of reproduction. They store the inherited qualities of one's parents. They are also in charge of growth and regulate body fluid.

The liver stores blood and is seen as the source of a person's emotional well-being and expression. In traditional Chinese medicine, the liver prefers to be cheerful and growing; it is averse to being gloomy and oppressed. Therefore, when the liver is inhibited by anger or depression, its Chi stagnates, which results in abnormal dispersion and emptying of blood. Ailment of the liver is usually viewed as a reason why a person suffers emotional distress and problems.

The spleen transforms and transports nutrients to all parts of the body. It is located in the left upper abdominal cavity, beneath the diaphragm and to the left of the stomach. When you focus Chi Kung practice in this area, you strengthen the spleen's function, increasing its transformation and transportation of nutrients, which results in an increase in appetite. It also strengthens the movement of the diaphragm, which produces a massaging effect on the stomach, promoting the contractions of its walls and aiding its digestive functions.

Chi Kung exercises also help channel what is known as the "small heavenly circuit of Chi" and the "large heavenly circuit of Chi." The small heavenly circuit refers to the circulation of Chi around the body along the *Ren* (front midline of the body) and *Du* (back midline of the body) meridians. Traditional Chinese medicine states that circulating Chi unimpeded through the Ren and Du meridians can get rid of hundreds of illnesses.

The large heavenly circuit of Chi functions on two levels. On one level, Chi is directed through the twelve physiological systems and their major visceral organs. On the second level, Chi from acupoints, such as the Dantian and *Baihui* (the center of the top of the head), is dispersed throughout the body without having to travel through the twelve systems first.

In the small heavenly circuit and both levels of the large heavenly circuit, the Chi that circulates in the body is intended to connect and interact with the Chi of the natural world.

# MEDICAL BENEFITS OF CHI KUNG

The Chi Kung exercises presented in this book can be practiced by anyone. The movements involved are not difficult, strenuous, or fast, and the mind plays an equally important role with the body. This makes Chi Kung a complete exercise for both the body and the mind. As you practice, you should begin to feel relaxed. When you practice it on a regular basis, Chi Kung can positively influence your breathing, heart, digestion, blood circulation, nervous system, metabolism, and many other bodily functions by working your Chi so that it keeps your body's biological processes in a steady and fluid motion. As a result, its main benefit is that it can help treat chronic disorders and even prevent illnesses by replenishing your body—removing what is old and replacing that with what is new.

## EFFECTS ON STRESS

Chi Kung practice is like meditation in which your mind and body movements work together so that you obtain a sense of harmony and a state of being centered. In order for your body to be relaxed, your mind must be clear and at ease, and one way to have a tranquil mind is to relax your body. A person's physical and mental functions are better when the body and mind are calm. The restful state of Chi Kung physiologically resembles sleep in many ways but it is actually very different from it. The person is calm but, at the same time, he or she is awake and alert and shows an increased reaction time, improved coordination, and better observation and hearing.

One of the main ways to achieving this restful state is the Chi Kung practice of taking long breaths. This makes the rate of your breathing decrease and the depth of your breathing deepen, which maximizes your intake of oxygen.

More oxygen is distributed to the tissues and organs of the body while more carbon dioxide is carried out by the circulating blood from the lungs and then exhaled. At the same time, you are bringing in the Chi from the natural world and, by concentrating, you help channel and focus it through your body so that you feel invigorated but centered. Correct posturing, proper movements, and clearing your mind of stray thoughts all help put you in a state of well-being. Your mind and body "slow down," reducing mental and physical tension.

When a person is under stress, his or her brain activities change. These activities can be recorded by an EEG (an electroencephalogram where electrodes are attached to different parts of the head). Research done with an EEG indicated that Chi Kung heightened the state of relaxation. During Chi Kung exercises, the subjects' brain showed an increase in the amount of time that the brain was emitting alpha and theta waves. This meant that the subjects in the research were awake yet completely relaxed.

Another way of measuring Chi Kung's calming effect is by using an electrocardiogram (EKG) to determine the skin's electrical potential at the subjects' acupoints. An EKG measures the electrical tension over the body through the surface of the skin. Subjects practicing Chi Kung were tested with an EKG and it showed that their acupoints' electrical potential was reduced while its temperature was raised. The subjects' Chi was actively flowing throughout their body while their excitability level was lessened.

## EFFECTS ON THE HEART

The practice of Chi Kung can help prevent heart disease, which is one of the leading causes of death in the Western world. It can regulate blood pressure and strengthen the heart by setting the body and mind at ease. In a relaxed state, heart rate decreases and less strain is placed on it. The mind focuses on the heart meridian so that the Chi around the heart flows more strongly and freely. This promotes a healthy circulation of blood which, in turn, helps prevent the formation of blocks of fat inside the blood vessels and reduces the size of the blockages that have already formed.

Heart disease can be detected by taking a person's blood sample and measuring the level of serum lipids. If the level is high, it is a probable sign of heart problem. In studies, people exercising Chi Kung over a period of time showed on average a reduced level of serum lipids. The subjects' total blood cholesterol (TC) and low-density lipoprotein cholesterol (LDL) were lower, while their high-density lipoprotein cholesterol (HDL) was higher. A low deposit of LDLs and an increase in HDL means a reduced risk of arteriosclerosis, a condition that lessens the elasticity of the walls of the arteries.

In a 1996 study at the Beijing Medical University, Dr. Ling Tan, a clinical professor, found that from Chi Kung practice patients with high blood pressure (ranging in age from 48 to 77) showed a decrease in blood pressure. Some 344 out of 422 patients decreased their diastolic blood pressure significantly (from a mean of 98 to a mean of 86 mmHg). In addition, 387 patients out of the 422 decreased their systolic blood pressure significantly (from a mean of 168 to a mean of 144 mmHg).

## EFFECTS ON THE IMMUNE SYSTEM

The most important findings in Chi Kung research in China today are its influences on the body's immune system. For years, immunologists were so busy exploring the complexity of the immune system that little attention was given to its communication with the other systems of the body. More recently, however, researchers have uncovered links between the mind and body by which psychophysiological mechanisms control the intimate communications between the nervous, endocrine, and immune systems. These immunologists have discovered that neurotransmitters from the nervous system and hormones from the endocrine system can attach themselves to immune cells and change their ability to multiply (by increasing or decreasing) and destroy invading agents.

Stress affects all parts of the body, including the immune system. There are basically three ways that the immune system can act: (1) depressed, (2) hyperactive, and (3) misguided.

A depressed or underactive immune systems occurs in response to certain hormones that are released from stress. As a result, a depressed immune system greatly increases the body's susceptibility to viruses.

A hyperactive immune system is caused by the secretion of other types of hormones that are products of stress. This hyperactive immune response seen in asthma patients is a highly irritable mucus lining of the lungs.

Similarly, autoimmune diseases, such as rheumatoid arthritis and lupus, are examples of a misguided immune system that attacks its own tissues as well as those of invading antigens.

Chi Kung exercises help put in balance and regulate the Yin and Yang in the body. Deep breathing helps to alleviate stress by calming the mind and body. At the same time, focused thoughts direct the Chi to certain acupoints that affect the different parts of the body; this promotes better circulation and, thus, improves strength. The acupoints that we will be concentrating on in this book are meant to provide an overall enhancement to the body (see Acupoints Commonly Used in Chi Kung, pp. 12–14).

# THREE KEY ELEMENTS OF CHI KUNG

Through the ages, Chi Kung masters have built up methods on how to practice Chi Kung the most effectively. These methods can be categorized as regulating the body, regulating breathing, and regulating the mind.

Regulating the body refers to the adjustment of body postures and relaxation exercises; regulating breathing refers to respiration exercises and the conducting of Chi; and regulating the mind refers to managing mental activities and exercising concentration and relaxation of the mind. These three key elements are completely dependent on one another. Combining and coordinating them are essential in practicing Chi Kung.

## REGULATING THE BODY

Chi Kung can be divided into two categories: dynamic Chi Kung and static Chi Kung. The former means practicing with motion while the latter is done without motion. Chi Kung can be exercised in many ways: lying down, sitting, and standing. The form of Chi Kung that we will focus on in this book is dynamic Chi Kung that is done standing up. The limbs and body are moved in ways that will help circulate and flow Chi. But before we can practice these movements, it is essential to assume the correct posture. This will guarantee smooth breathing and produce a mentally relaxed state. The theory is that if your posture is not correct, then your flow of Chi cannot be smooth; if your flow of Chi is not smooth, then your mind cannot concentrate; if your mind cannot concentrate, then your Chi will be in disorder.

**Feet and Knees**   Start by adjusting your feet parallel to each other about 3–4 feet-width apart or whatever distance makes you feel balanced. Keep your knees slightly bent so that you are steady and grounded to the earth. How much

you bend your knees determines your standing form—whether it is high, middle, or low. Your stance provides the foundation for the rest of your body.

**Head and Neck**   Keep your head and neck naturally straight. In traditional Chinese medicine, the Baihui is considered the "meeting place of one hundred meridians." Here, at the center of the top of the head, the energy field opens, so it is important that you allow Chi to flow unimpeded. Your neck is the passageway for most major nerves, blood vessels, and Chi between your head and the rest of your body. It is essential that you keep it upright as well, so that you permit the proper circulation.

**Eyes**   Look straight ahead or slightly close your eyes so that you can concentrate and not be distracted by what is happening around you.

**Mouth and Tongue**   Naturally close your mouth and keep your lower jaw slightly drawn in. Raise the tip of your tongue against the upper palate of your mouth so that it is naturally curled and relaxed. This helps to better circulate the Chi in your body. Put a slight smile on your face.

**Torso**   Ease your shoulders so that they naturally hang and the muscles associated with your upper back are relaxed. Slightly draw in your chest and abdomen to help you keep your back naturally erect and your spine upright. It is important that your body be aligned correctly so that your center of gravity is balanced and your Chi flows freely. Relax your waist and hips so that your Chi will grow in your Dantian and, from there, travel to all the parts of your body, creating a sense of harmony.

**Arms**   Place your arms in front of you and bend your elbows as if you are hugging someone. Keep your fingers loose, naturally separated, and slightly bent as if you are holding a ball. Point your fingertips downward and hold your palms inward. The gesture of your arms and fingers creates a circle so that Chi travels through both arms.

## REGULATING BREATHING

Regulating your breathing is an important link to training and directing your Chi. With each breath, Chi is being gathered, initiated, and circulated throughout the body. When you are exercising breathing, as you inhale image the Chi from the natural world going in through your nose to your chest, then abdomen, and finally Dantian. When breathing out, image the Chi going out from your Dantian to your arms, forearms, hands, palms, fingers, then thighs, legs, feet, toes, and finally outside your body. Image the Chi moving through the meridians of your body, connecting your body to the natural world.

There are two common methods of regulating your breathing. The first method involves lowering your diaphragm while extending your abdomen as you inhale. As you exhale, draw up your diaphragm and pull in your abdomen. The second method is the reversal of the first and the way we normally breathe. As you inhale, draw up your diaphragm and draw in your abdomen. As you exhale, lower your diaphragm and extend your abdomen. Regardless of which method you use, always coordinate it with your body movements and mind exercises.

## REGULATING THE MIND

Setting your thoughts into a correct mind-set to achieve a state of relaxation is the most essential key to exercising Chi Kung. This practice is known as "training the mind to return to the void" or being in a Chi Kung state. The "void" is comparable to meditation, in which the goal is to reach a spiritual inner peace. The effectiveness of your Chi Kung practice is mainly determined by how relaxed you are. It may at first be difficult for beginners to achieve this state of relaxation, but the more you practice it, the easier it will eventually be.

To obtain a Chi Kung state you need to go through these series of stages: You must first get rid of all stray thoughts. Concentrate and focus your mind on a certain part of your body or a certain acupoint. Your Dantian is usually a good place to start. From your Dantian, let your mind flow to the other parts of your body—your breathing, your diaphragm rising and falling, your heartbeat, your circulating Chi, and your body movements. Gradually, you will achieve complete and deep relaxation and enter a state of "void" where a sense of harmony is within you and between you and the natural world.

# ACUPOINTS COMMONLY USED IN CHI KUNG

There are hundreds of acupoints located throughout the human body. The Chi Kung exercises in this book focuses on several essential ones. As you do the different exercises, you will concentrate on the relevant acupoints by imaging Chi circulating through them.

A *cun* is the standard unit of measurement for locating acupoints. One cun is equivalent to the width of the middle joint of your thumb (see Figure 1). Three cuns is the width of the index, middle, ring, and pinkie fingers closed together. The measurement is taken along the line of the middle joint of the middle finger (see Figure 2).

Each acupoint mentioned below has a standard meridian abbreviation indicating which meridian that acupoint is associated with: GV, Governing Vessel; SP, Spleen; Extra or EX, Extra Point; ST, Stomach; PC, Pericardium; KI, Kidney.

**Baihui (GV 20):** The center of the top of the head, 7 cun directly above the bottom hairline (see Figure 3). This acupoint helps relieve headaches, clears the mind, and promotes relaxation, memory, and concentration.

**Fengfu (GV 16):** Located on 1 cun directly above the bottom hairline (see Figure 3). This acupoint helps relieve headaches, neck pains, nosebleeds, and sore throats. It also helps clear the head and nose and promotes blood circulation.

**Dabao (SP 21):** Located 6 cun below the joint where the forearm meets the body (see Figure 4). This acupoint helps relieve chest discomfort or pain and abdominal pain.

**Yintang (EX-HN3):** Between the eyebrows where the bridge of the nose joins the forehead (see Figure 5). This acupoint helps lower blood pressure, promotes relaxation, and stimulates immune functions.

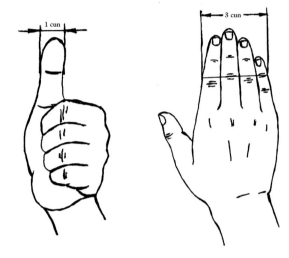

**Figure 1.** 1 cun.      **Figure 2.** 3 cun.

**Qihu (ST 13):** Located at the lower border of the middle of the clavicle, 4 cun across the midline of the body (see Figure 5). This acupoint helps relieve chest congestion, coughs, stiff neck, swollen and sore throats.

**Dantian (Extra):** Located along the imaginary line joining the navel and pubic bone about one-third of the way down from the navel and two-thirds up from the pubic bone (see Figure 5). This acupoint helps strengthen the lower back and helps replenish Chi in the body.

**Dazhui (GV 14):** Located in the cavity right below the seventh vertebra of the neck vertebrae (see Figure 6). This acupoints helps strengthen breathing, relieve fever, chest congestion, arm and back pain, stiff neck.

**Mingmen (GV 4):** Located in the cavity below the second vertebra of the second lumbar (hip) vertebrae (see Figure 6). It is 1 cun above the buttocks in the midline of the body. It helps relieve backaches, ringing in the ears, hard of hearing, diarrhea, and it helps strengthen the bladder.

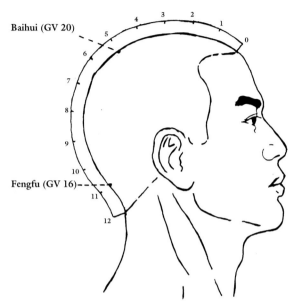

Figure 3. Baihui and Fengfu.

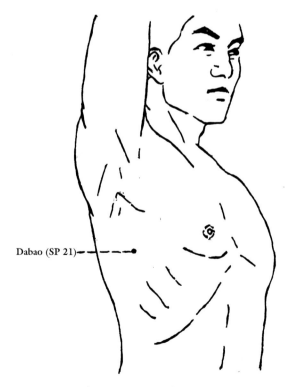

Figure 4. Dabao.

**Laogong (PC 8):** Between the bones of the second and middle fingers, slightly below the middle crease of the palm. In a clenched fist, the acupoint is just below the tip of the middle finger (see Figure 7). This acupoint helps relieve shaky hands, feelings of faintness and convulsion, and swollen and sore throats.

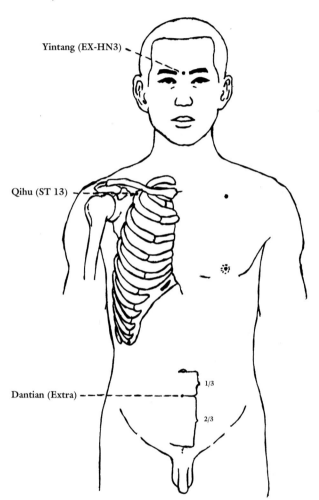

Figure 5. Yintang, Qihu, and Dantian.

**Yongquan (KI 1):** Located on the sole of the foot about a third down from the end of the second toe and two-thirds of the way up from the heel of the foot (see Figure 8). It is the indentation formed when the toes are curled under. This acupoint promotes relaxation and blood circulation.

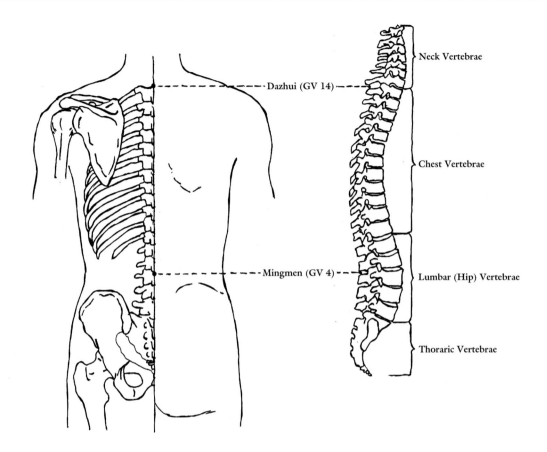

**Figure 6.** Dazhui and Mingmen.

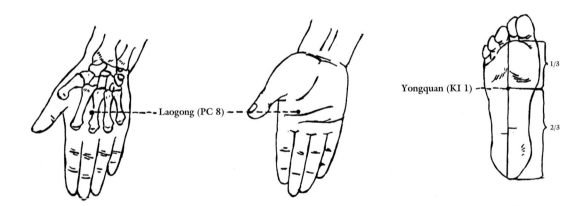

**Figure 7.** Laogong.

**Figure 8**. Yongquan.

# PRACTICING CHI KUNG

When practicing Chi Kung, remember to combine the elements of mind, breathing, and body movement. The best way to practice is to use this book with the guide of a master or an experienced teacher. If you cannot find a teacher, this book has all the essential information. It contains six sequences of five or more forms. Each movement has a photograph with arrows to show the direction of the movement and text explaining how you should move, breathe, and what your mind should be focusing on. It takes about 20 minutes to complete the whole exercise of the entire six sequences. All the movements should be done continuously unless otherwise specified.

Don't rush through the movements, because it will only spoil the sense of harmony, self-reflection, and relaxation that you are trying to create. One of the goals of Chi Kung is to balance the mind and body. The more you practice and understand this purpose, the richer your mental and physical experiences will be. As you go through the sequences in this book, you may feel various sensations. These sensations are normal in Chi Kung practice and they are usually the result of the Chi, which was stagnant before, and is now flowing vigorously throughout your body. Let's explore these sensations before we begin practicing Chi Kung.

## FEELINGS OF CHI

**Seven Touches:** During Chi Kung exercises, your body can experience what is known as the "seven touches." They are feelings of largeness, smallness, lightness, heaviness, cold, heat, and tingling of the skin.

When your body is in a relaxed state, Chi circulates freely and the blood vessels in your body tend to expand, giving you the feeling of being very tall and large. When Chi is gathered at the Dantian, you will have the sensation of having a very small body.

A feeling of lightness can happen when Chi goes through your Ren and Du meridians and reaches your Baihui. You may feel that your movements are slow and smooth, as if you are not touching the ground—like an astronaut on the moon. In contrast, Chi sinking down into your Yongquan in both feet when you exhale will give you the feeling that you are as heavy as a rock—so solid that nothing can move you.

When Chi circulates through the heavenly circuits of your body, balancing the functions of your heart and kidneys so that your body fluid is in equilibrium, you may experience a pleasantly cool sensation, whereas Chi that flows vigorously produces a hot sensation. The lower abdomen and four limbs are the most common places where you will feel warmth. In some cases, you may even perspire a bit.

If you feel any tingling or itching sensation, it is because the meridians in your body, which were obstructed at ordinary times, are now free, with Chi passing through them.

As you continue with your practice all these feelings will quickly disappear.

**Seeing Light:** Once you've reached a certain level of the Chi Kung state you may see flashes of light that appear like lightning coming to and from the light source of where you're practicing. Other times the light may seem to be piercing into your brain behind your eyes through your spinal column, and sometimes there may appear a ball of light rotating at high speed through the Ren and Du meridians of your body. Your spinal column, Ren and Du meridians, and Baihui are all connected and communicate with each other. When Chi goes through the Ren and Du meridians or spinal column, it reaches the Baihui of your head, which gives you the sensation of light. The degree and color of light varies according to the level of the Chi Kung state. These phenomena are only temporary and will disappear instantaneously.

There are instances, however, where people have achieved such a high level of Chi Kung state that a ball of light or light beam may constantly exist at the Baihui. This level is difficult to achieve and is usually only accomplished by Chi Kung masters or experts.

**Hunger:** During Chi Kung practice, as Chi flows vigorously through your body it helps to stimulate the activities of the different organs and strengthen circulation. Your diaphragm actively moves with each concentrated breath, rubbing your stomach and stimulating the contraction of its walls. All these activities increase your body's function, which can make you feel hungry.

**Vigorous Spirit:** You can be in a state of tranquility and freshness for a good period of time after practice. Your body has been replenished—turbid Chi has been expelled and essential Chi from the natural world has been brought in. Tension and pent-up emotions have been released, and your mind has found a sense of balance with your body.

## BEFORE YOU BEGIN

Find a quiet and peaceful place outdoors, such as a park, with good light, fresh air, and attractive scenery, so that you can be in a good spirit and breathe in the Chi from the heaven and earth. If the weather outside is not good, try to find a suitable indoor place that is clean, bright, quiet, and has circulating fresh air.

Wear clothes that are comfortable, loose-fitting, and soft in color. A nice sweatshirt and pair of sweatpants are ideal. Make sure that you are well rested. If you feel tired or stressed, try to rest, take a relaxing bath, or, if possible, get a massage. It is important that you feel at your best.

Relieve your bladder. Concentrate and relax.

## DURING PRACTICE

Think about the form that you are exercising. Think about the direction in which you are standing. Normally, you should face south with your back facing north. We believe that Chi from the natural world travels from south to north. By facing south, it is easier to connect your internal Chi with the outside Chi. Take several deep breaths, relax your body, and free your mind of stray thoughts while concentrating on your Dantian.

Your breathing should be natural, free and smooth, slow and gentle, and coordinate with your thoughts and body movement to help you reach a state of relaxation. There are two kind of breathing to keep in mind during Chi Kung practice: training and nourishing. Training refers to training and strengthening your Chi through concentration during Chi Kung practice; while nourishing refers to replenishing your vigor and energy after practice. Chi Kung masters have remarked that "vigorous breathing is training, gentle breathing is nourishing."

Chi Kung exercises are not practiced through to the end with one form of breathing, but by alternating between one and the other. For instance, if you feel tired while practicing, concentrate on your Dantian and breathe freely until you relax. Alternating between training and nourishing breathing can enhance the quality of your practice.

As you reach a Chi Kung state, you may feel the effects of Chi. Any hot, cold, or tingling sensations will lessen naturally. Any flash of light that may appear before your eyes is only temporary. Remain relaxed and focused.

If the amount of saliva in your mouth increases, swallow it three times to be sure that you swallow it all. Don't spit it out because, in traditional Chinese medicine, saliva is very important in digesting food and nurturing the organ systems within the body.

If at any time during the practice you feel uncomfortable in your posture, correct yourself until you feel right.

## CLOSING PRACTICE

Close your practice by imagine your Chi going to your Dantian. Take several deep breaths and open your eyes slowly. Go for a walk and take several deep breaths again. Stretch out your back, arms, and legs. Remain quiet and reflective for a while as the feelings of Chi subside, before you start any other activities.

# FIRST SEQUENCE
# (1-11)

## (1) Preparation

*Yu Bei Shi*

**Movement 1:** Stand with your feet about a shoulder-width apart. Let your arms hang naturally. Keep your head raised as if balancing a book. Have your spine erect, knees slightly bent, and toes firmly touching the ground. The tip of the tongue should be raised against the hard palate with the mouth slightly closed. Look straight ahead without focusing on anything. Get rid of any stray thoughts, relax, and breathe evenly and deeply. Concentrate on the Dantian and stand still for 3–5 minutes. Slowly lower your eyelids until your eyes are slightly closed. (See photo 1.) The arrows in the photos indicate the direction of the next movement.
**Breathing:** Inhale and exhale several times.
**Mind:** Concentrate on the Dantian.

**Movement 2:** Slowly raise your arms slightly with the fingers of both hands pointing forward. (See photo 2.)
**Breathing:** Inhale.
**Mind:** Concentrate on the Dantian.

*continued next page*

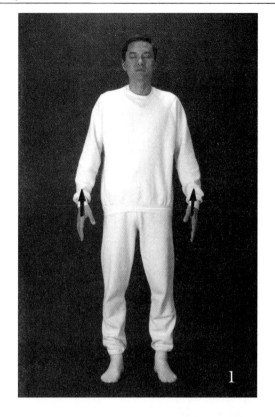

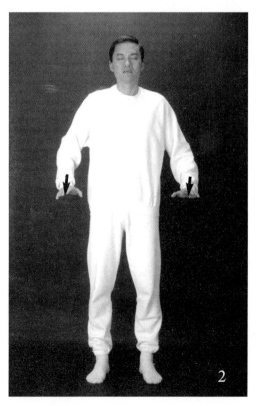

**Movement 3:** Then press down your palms. (See photo 3.)
**Breathing:** Inhale.
**Mind:** Concentrate on the Dantian.

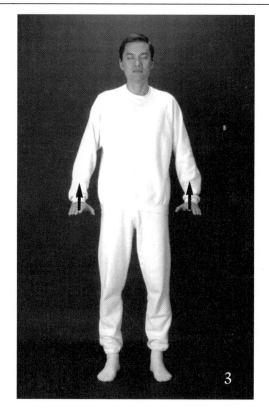

## (2) Draw Chi from the Earth 1

### *Di Xia La Qi 1*

**Movement 1:** Stand relaxed and with both arms naturally hanging down, the palms facing downward, and fingers of each hand slightly tightened up. Move your hands forward and your palms upward until they are about 45 degrees from your body and reach the level of the Dantian. (See photo 4.)

**Breathing:** Inhale.

**Mind:** Imagine Chi from the earth reaching your Laogong, then going from your palms to arms, and finally to your Dantian.

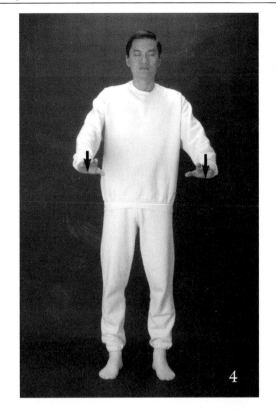

**Movement 2:** Move your hands down and back with a slight tension until they are in their original position at both sides of the body. (See photo 5.)

**Breathing:** Exhale.

**Mind:** Imagine Chi going from your Dantian to your arms, then palms, and from your Laogong to the earth.

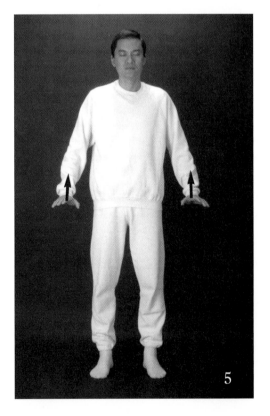

# (3) Draw Chi from the Earth 2

## *Di Xia La Qi 2*

**Movement 1:** Stand relaxed and with both arms naturally hanging down, the palms facing downward, and fingers of each hand slightly tightened up. Move your hands forward and your palms upward until they are about 45 degrees from your body and reach the level of the Dantian. (See photo 6.)

**Breathing:** Inhale.

**Mind:** Imagine Chi from the earth reaching your Laogong, then going from your palms to arms, and finally to your Dantian.

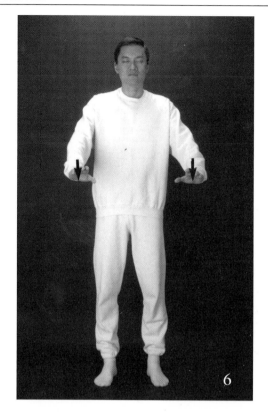

**Movement 2:** Move your hands down and back with a slight tension until they are in their original position at both sides of the body. (See photo 7.)

**Breathing:** Exhale.

**Mind:** Imagine Chi going from your Dantian to your arms, then palms, and from your Laogong to the earth.

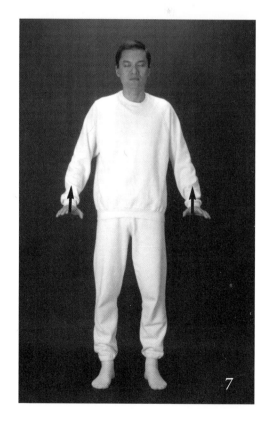

## (4) Draw Chi from the Earth 3

*Di Xia La Qi 3*

**Movement 1:** Stand relaxed and with both arms naturally hanging down, the palms facing downward, and fingers of each hand slightly tightened up. Move your hands forward and your palms upward until they are about 45 degrees from your body and reach the level of the Dantian. (See photo 8.)

**Breathing:** Inhale.

**Mind:** Imagine Chi from the earth reaching your Laogong, then going from your palms to arms, and finally to your Dantian.

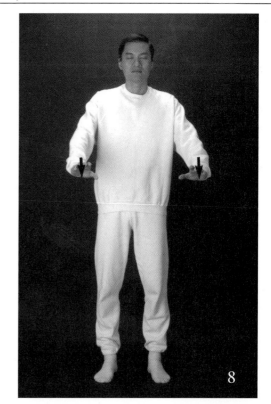

**Movement 2:** Move your hands down and back with a slight tension until they are in their original position at both sides of the body. (See photo 9.)

**Breathing:** Exhale.

**Mind:** Imagine Chi going from your Dantian to your arms, then palms, and from your Laogong to the earth.

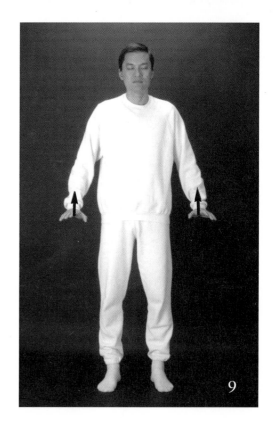

# (5) Direct Chi to Dantian

*Yin Qi Dao Dantian*

**Movement 1:** Turn both palms inward and lift them up to the level of your Dantian in front of your body. (See photo 10.)

**Breathing:** Inhale.

**Mind:** Imagine Chi being held between your two palms.

**Movement 2:** Turn both palms to face your Dantian and then press them toward the Dantian with a slight tension as if you are embracing someone. Hold for 2 to 3 seconds. (See photo 11.)

**Breathing:** Exhale.

**Mind:** Imagine Chi going into your Dantian from your two palms.

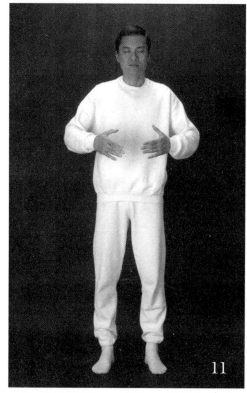

## (6) Direct Chi to Mingmen

### *Yin Qi Dao Mingmen*

**Movement 1:** Turn both palms to face downward and then draw both hands outward until they are at the two sides of your body. Continue drawing them back until they almost reach each other in the back of your body at the level of Mingmen. (See photos 12 and 13.)

**Breathing:** Inhale.

**Mind:** Imagine Chi being held in both palms.

**Movement 2:** Press both palms toward your Mingmen with a slight tension. (See photo 14.)

**Breathing:** Exhale.

**Mind:** Imagine Chi going into your Mingmen from both palms.

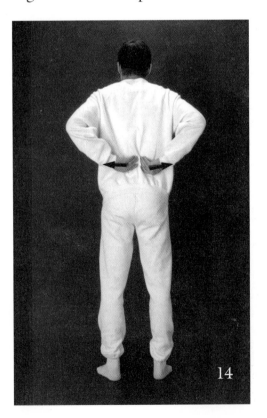

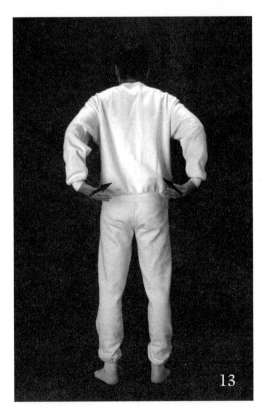

## (7) Direct Chi to Dabao

*Yin Qi Dao Dabao*

**Movement 1:** Turn both palms upward, then move them to the front of the body and under the armpits. (See photo 15.)
**Breathing:** Inhale.
**Mind:** Imagine Chi being held in both palms.

**Movement 2:** Press your middle fingers toward the Dabao with a slight tension. (See photo 16.)
**Breathing:** Exhale.
**Mind:** Imagine Chi going from your palms through your middle fingers into your Dabao.

# (8) Direct Chi to Yintang

## *Yin Qi Dao Yintang*

**Movement 1:** Turn both palms upward, bring both hands forward with strength focused on the ends of the middle fingers and with the portion of the palms at the base of the thumb slightly pressing down at the level of the Yintang. (See photo 17.)

**Breathing:** Inhale.

**Mind:** Imagine Chi being held by the two palms.

**Movement 2:** Turn both palms toward the face, then press them toward the Yintang with a slight tension. Hold for 2 to 3 seconds. (See photo 18.)

**Breathing:** Exhale.

**Mind:** Imagine Chi going from both palms to the Yintang.

# (9) Separate Hands

*Liang Shou Feng Kai*

**Movement 1:** Keep both palms inward, then draw your hands and arms outward until they are at shoulder level. (See photo 19.)

**Breathing:** Inhale.

**Mind:** Imagine Chi coming from the sky and being held in both palms.

**Movement 2:** Turn both palms upward and bend both elbows slightly. (See photo 20.)

**Breathing:** Exhale.

**Mind:** Imagine Chi going out from both palms.

## (10) Direct Chi to Baihui

*Yin Qi Dao Baihui*

**Movement 1:** Raise both hands upward until they reach overhead. Palms should be facing inward. (See photo 21.)

**Breathing:** Inhale.

**Mind:** Imagine Chi being held in both palms.

**Movement 2:** Press both palms toward the Baihui with a slight tension. Hold for 2 to 3 seconds. (See photo 22.)

**Breathing:** Exhale.

**Mind:** Imagine Chi going from both palms to the Baihui.

# (11) Press Palms in Front of the Chest

*Xiong Qian He Zhang*

**Movement 1:** Press both palms together overhead with a slight tension. (See photo 23.)
**Breathing:** Inhale.
**Mind:** Imagine Chi being held in both palms.

23

**Movement 2:** Move both hands forward and downward until they reach chest level. Lightly press the palms together with the fingers turned upward and the tips of the thumbs pointing at the chest. (See photo 24.)
**Breathing:** Exhale.
**Mind:** Imagine Chi going out from the fingers and thumbs to the sky.

24

# SECOND SEQUENCE (12–28)

## (12) Get Chi from the Edge of the Sky

*Tian Bian De Qi*

**Movement 1:** Keeping the two palms pressed together, extend your arms and fingers forward until your shoulders, elbows, and wrists form a straight line. (See photo 25.)
**Breathing:** Inhale.
**Mind:** Imagine that the two palms are reaching the edge of the sky and that Chi is coming into them from the sky.

25

**Movement 2:** Open up your palms so that they face forward and stand vertically. Keeping the fingers of both hands together, join both thumbs and index fingers so that you form a triangle. (See photo 26.)
**Breathing:** Exhale.
**Mind:** Imagine Chi going out of the triangle between the two palms.

26

## (13) Separate Hands

*Liang Shou Feng Kai*

**Movement 1:** Keeping your two palms up, separate both hands outward until they are at shoulder-width. (See photo 27.)
**Breathing:** Inhale.
**Mind:** Imagine Chi going into the two palms from the edge of the sky.

**Movement 2:** Push both palms slightly forward. (See photo 28.)
**Breathing:** Exhale.
**Mind:** Imagine Chi going from both palms back out to the sky.

31

# (14) Get Chi from the Front Side of the Sky 1

### *Zheng Qian Mian De Qi 1*

**Movement 1:** Pull both hands back until your elbows are at 90 degrees. (See photo 29.)

**Breathing:** Inhale.

**Mind:** Imagine Chi going from the front edge of sky into both palms.

**Movement 2:** Keeping the palms up, push both hands slightly forward until the elbows are straight. (See photo 30.)

**Breathing:** Exhale.

**Mind:** Imagine the two palms reaching the front edge of the sky and Chi going out from them.

## (15) Get Chi from the Front Side of the Sky 2

*Zheng Qian Mian De Qi 2*

**Movement 1:** Pull both hands back until your elbows are at 90 degrees. (See photo 31.)

**Breathing:** Inhale.

**Mind:** Imagine Chi going from the front edge of the sky into both palms.

**Movement 2:** Keeping the palms up, push both hands forward until the elbows are straight. (See photo 32.)

**Breathing:** Exhale.

**Mind:** Imagine the two palms reaching the front edge of the sky and Chi going out from them.

## (16) Get Chi from the Front Side of the Sky 3

### *Zheng Qian Mian De Qi 3*

**Movement 1:** Pull both hands back until your elbows are at 90 degrees. (See photo 33.)

**Breathing:** Inhale.

**Mind:** Imagine Chi going from the front edge of the sky into both palms.

**Movement 2:** Keeping the palms up, push both hands forward until your elbows are straight. (See photo 34.)

**Breathing:** Exhale.

**Mind:** Imagine the two palms reaching the front edge of the sky and Chi going out from them.

## (17) Get Chi from the Inner Left and Right Front Sides of the Sky 1

*Nei Ce Qian De Qi 1*

**Movement 1:** Keeping your palms and fingers up, separate both hands outward until they are 45 degrees from the body. (See photo 35.)

**Breathing:** Inhale.

**Mind:** Imagine Chi going from the left and right front sides of the sky into both palms.

35

**Movement 2:** Bring both hands back inward until they are a shoulder-width apart. (See photo 36.)

**Breathing:** Exhale.

**Mind:** Imagine Chi going out from both palms.

36

## (18) Get Chi from the Inner Left and Right Front Sides of the Sky 2

*Nei Ce Qian De Qi 2*

**Movement 1:** Keeping both palms and fingers up, move both hands outward again until they are 45 degrees from the body. (See photo 37.)

**Breathing:** Inhale.

**Mind:** Imagine Chi going from the left and right front sides of the sky into both palms.

37

**Movement 2:** Bring both hands back inward until they are a shoulder-width apart. (See photo 38.)

**Breathing:** Exhale.

**Mind:** Imagine Chi going out from both palms.

38

# (19) Get Chi from the Inner Left and Right Front Sides of the Sky 3

*Nei Ce Qian De Qi 3*

**Movement 1:** Keeping both palms and fingers up, move both hands outward again until they are 45 degrees from the body. (See photo 39.)

**Breathing:** Inhale.

**Mind:** Imagine Chi going from the left and right front sides of the sky into both palms.

**Movement 2:** Bring both hands inward until they are a shoulder-width apart. (See photo 40.)

**Breathing:** Exhale.

**Mind:** Imagine Chi going out from both palms.

## (20) Stretch Hands Like a Bird's Wings

*Fen Niao Chi Bang*

**Movement 1:** Keeping palms and fingers up, stretch out both arms to the sides of the body just as a bird stretches out its wings. (See photo 41.)

**Breathing:** Inhale.

**Mind:** Imagine Chi going from the right and left sides into their respective palms.

**Movement 2:** Push out both arms until the elbows are straight. Keep the fingers and palms up. (See photo 42.)

**Breathing:** Exhale.

**Mind:** Imagine Chi going out from both palms.

## (21) Pull Chi from the Left and Right Sides of the Sky 1

*Zuo You De Qi 1*

**Movement 1:** Keeping both hands pointing out to the sides, pull them toward your shoulder until the elbows are at a 90-degree angle. (See photo 43.)
**Breathing:** Inhale.
**Mind:** Image Chi going from the left and right sides of the sky into both palms.

**Movement 2:** Push both arms out until the elbows are straight again. (See photo 44.)
**Breathing:** Exhale.
**Mind:** Imagine Chi going out from both palms.

## (22) Pull Chi from the Left and Right Sides of the Sky 2

*Zuo You De Qi 2*

**Movement 1:** Keeping both hands pointing out to the sides, pull them toward your shoulder until the elbows are at a 90-degree angle. (See photo 45.)
**Breathing:** Inhale.
**Mind:** Image Chi going from the left and right sides of the sky into both palms.

**Movement 2:** Push hands out until the elbows are straight again. (See photo 46.)
**Breathing:** Exhale.
**Mind:** Imagine Chi going out from both palms.

## (23) Pull Chi from the Left and Right Sides of the Sky 3

*Zuo You De Qi 3*

**Movement 1:** Keeping both hands pointing out to the sides, pull them toward your shoulders until the elbows are at a 90-degree angle. (See photo 47.)

**Breathing:** Inhale.

**Mind:** Image Chi going from the left and right sides of the sky into both palms.

**Movement 2:** Push hands outward until the elbows are straight again. (See photo 48.)

**Breathing:** Exhale.

**Mind:** Imagine Chi going out from both palms.

## (24) Get Chi from the Left and Right Upper Sides of the Sky 1

*Zuo You Shang Ce De Qi 1*

**Movement 1:** Keeping both palms and fingers up, move both hands upward 45 degrees. (See photo 49.)
**Breathing:** Inhale.
**Mind:** Imagine Chi going from the left and right upper sides of the sky into both palms.

**Movement 2:** Move both hands downward until they reach shoulder level. (See photo 50.)
**Breathing:** Exhale.
**Mind:** Imagine Chi going from the two palms out to both sides of the sky.

# (25) Get Chi from the Left and Right Upper Sides of the Sky 2

*Zuo You Shang Ce De Qi 2*

**Movement 1:** Keeping both palms and fingers up, move both hands upward 45 degrees. (See photo 51.)
**Breathing:** Inhale.
**Mind:** Imagine Chi going from the left and right upper sides of the sky into both palms.

**Movement 2:** Move both hands downward until they reach shoulder level. (See photo 52.)
**Breathing:** Exhale.
**Mind:** Imagine Chi going from the two palms out to both sides of the sky.

## (26) Get Chi from the Left and Right Upper Sides of the Sky 3

*Zuo You Shang Ce De Qi 3*

**Movement 1:** Keeping both palms and fingers up, move both hands upward 45 degrees. (See photo 53.)
**Breathing:** Inhale.
**Mind:** Imagine Chi going from the left and right upper sides of the sky into both palms.

**Movement 2:** Move both hands downward until they reach shoulder level. (See photo 54.)
**Breathing:** Exhale.
**Mind:** Imagine Chi going from the two palms out to both sides of the sky.

## (27) Direct Chi to Baihui

*Ying Qi Dao Baihui*

**Movement 1:** Turn both palms inward but facing up. Raise your arms upward until your hands are over your head. (See photo 55.)
**Breathing:** Inhale.
**Mind:** Imagine Chi being held in both palms.

55

**Movement 2:** Press both palms toward your Baihui with a slight tension. Hold for 2 to 3 seconds. (See photo 56.)
**Breathing:** Exhale.
**Mind:** Imagine Chi going from both palms into your Baihui.

56

# (28) Direct Chi to Dantian

*Ying Qi Dao Dantian*

**Movement 1:** Bring your hands down and let your palms pass in front of your face, neck, chest, and abdomen. Stop in front of your Dantian. (See photos 57 and 58.)

**Breathing:** Inhale.

**Mind:** Imagine Chi going between both palms to the face, neck, chest, and abdomen.

**Movement 2:** Use both middle fingers to gently press your Dantian. (See photo 59.)

**Breathing:** Exhale.

**Mind:** Imagine Chi going from both middle fingers into your Dantian.

57

59

58

# THIRD SEQUENCE
# (29–35)

## (29) Direct Chi to Mingmen

*Ying Qi Dao Mingmen*

**Movement 1:** Place your palms on both sides of your abdomen, then move both palms backward until they reach your back at the level of Mingmen. (See photos 60 and 61.)

**Breathing:** Inhale.

**Mind:** Imagine Chi going between both palms through both sides of your abdomen and back.

**Movement 2:** Press both your middle fingers gently into your Mingmen. (See photo 62.)

**Breathing:** Exhale.

**Mind:** Imagine Chi going from both middle fingers into the Mingmen.

60

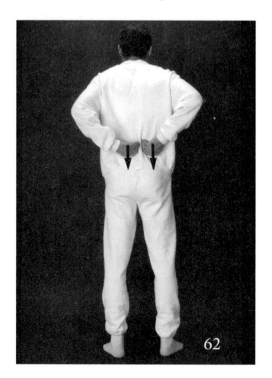

62

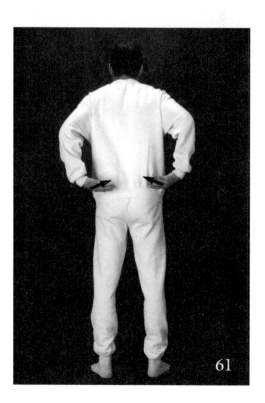

61

# (30) Direct Chi to Yongquan

*Ying Qi Dao Yongquan*

**Movement 1:** Bend forward slowly, keeping your legs and knees straight while your arms are hanging down. Slide both palms from your buttocks to the back side of your thighs, then to your legs and to the left and right sides of your feet. As you slide down, bend your knees as needed. Stop at your toes. (See photo 63.)

**Breathing:** Inhale.

**Mind:** Imagine Chi going between both palms through the buttocks, the back side of thighs, legs, left and right sides of feet, and finally toes.

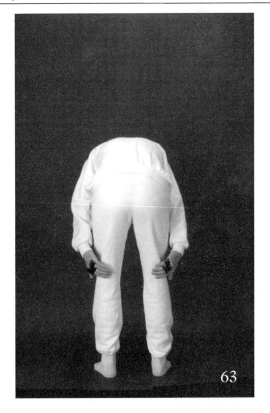

63

**Movement 2:** Press both palms gently over your toes. (See photo 64.)

**Breathing:** Exhale.

**Mind:** Imagine Chi going from both palms to your Yongquan.

64

# (31) Connect Chi Between Dantian and Yongquan 1

*Lian Jie Dantian Yongquan 1*

**Movement 1:** Lift your hands up off your toes as you bring up your body and straighten your knees. Stop when your hands reach the level of your knees. (See photo 65.)

**Breathing:** Inhale.

**Mind:** Imagine Chi coming from the earth to your Yongquan, then going through both feet, legs, thighs to your Dantian.

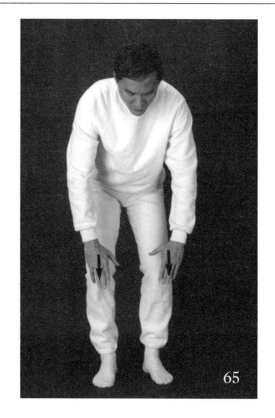

**Movement 2:** Move your body back down and bend your knees until both palms are pressing your toes. (See photo 66.)

**Breathing:** Exhale.

**Mind:** Imagine Chi coming from your Dantian through your thighs, legs, feet, and then from your Yongquan to the earth.

## (32) Connect Chi Between Dantian and Yongquan 2

*Lian Jie Dantian Yongquan 2*

**Movement 1:** Lift your hands up off your toes as you bring up your body and straighten your knees. Stop when your hands reach the level of your knees. (See photo 67.)

**Breathing:** Inhale.

**Mind:** Imagine Chi coming from the earth to your Yongquan, then going through both feet, legs, and thighs to your Dantian.

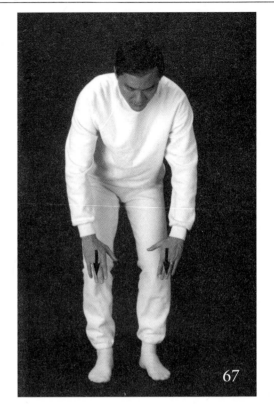

**Movement 2:** Move your body back down and bend your knees until both palms are pressing your toes. (See photo 68.)

**Breathing:** Exhale.

**Mind:** Imagine Chi coming from your Dantian through thighs, legs, feet, and then going from your Yongquan to the earth.

# (33) Connect Chi Between Dantian and Yongquan 3

*Lian Jie Dantian Yongquan 3*

**Movement 1:** Lift your hands up off your toes as you bring up your body and straighten your knees. Stop when your hands reach the level of your knees. (See photo 67.)

**Breathing:** Inhale.

**Mind:** Imagine Chi coming from the earth to your Yongquan, then going through both feet, legs, and thighs to your Dantian.

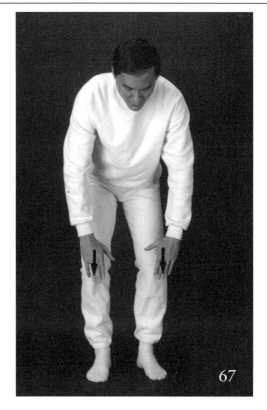

67

**Movement 2:** Move your body back down and bend your knees until both palms are pressing your toes. (See photo 68.)

**Breathing:** Exhale.

**Mind:** Imagine Chi coming from your Dantian through thighs, legs, feet, and then going from your Yongquan to the earth.

68

51

# (34) Draw Chi to Dantian

*Ying Qi Dao Dantian*

**Movement 1:** Bring your body slowly back up as your straighten your knees and waist. Slide both palms over the top of your feet, then in front of your legs, thighs, waist, abdomen, and stop in front of your Dantian. (See photos 69 and 70).

**Breathing:** Inhale.

**Mind:** Imagine Chi coming from your Yongquan, then going between both palms and the inside of your feet, front side of legs, thighs, waist, abdomen, and finally your Dantian.

**Movement 2:** Press both middle fingers gently on your Dantian. (See photo 71.)

**Breathing:** Exhale.

**Mind:** Imagine Chi going into the Dantian.

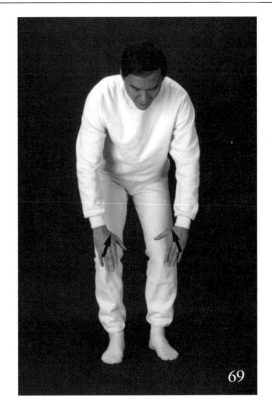

69

71

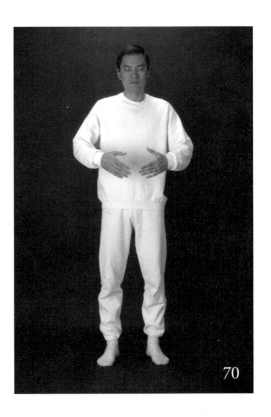

70

# (35) Bring Chi Back to the Earth

## *Qi Qui Di Qiu*

**Movement 1:** Move your hands away from your Dantian and bring them down to the sides of your body. Let your hands hang down naturally. (See photo 72.)

**Breathing:** Inhale.

**Mind:** Imagine Chi going from your Dantian to both palms.

**Movement 2:** Press both palms slightly downward and point your fingers forward. (See photo 72.)

**Breathing:** Exhale.

**Mind:** Imagine Chi going from both palms back to the earth.

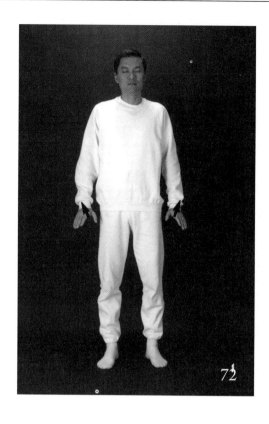
72

# FOURTH SEQUENCE
## (36–55)

## (36) Raise Hands Like a Bird's Wings

*Ti Shou Si Niao Chi Bang*

**Movement 1:** Raise your arms and hands until they are at shoulder level. Bend both elbows slightly. (See photo 73.)
**Breathing:** Inhale.
**Mind:** Imagine Chi going from your Dantian to both palms.

73

**Movement 2:** Raise both hands with fingers pointing upward, then push both palms slightly outward. (See photo 74.)
**Breathing:** Exhale.
**Mind:** Imagine Chi going out from both palms.

74

## (37) Get Chi from the Left and Right Sides of the Sky 4

*Zuo You De Qi 4*

**Movement 1:** Keeping both hands pointing out to the sides, pull them toward your shoulder until the elbows are at a 90-degree angle. (See photo 75.)

**Breathing:** Inhale.

**Mind:** Imagine Chi going from both sides of the sky into both palms.

**Movement 2:** Push both arms out until your elbows are straight. (See photo 76.)

**Breathing:** Exhale.

**Mind:** Imagine Chi going out from both palms.

## (38) Get Chi from the Left and Right Sides of the Sky 5

*Zuo You De Qi 5*

**Movement 1:** Keeping both hands pointing out to the sides, pull them toward your shoulder until the elbows are at a 90-degree angle. (See photo 77.)
**Breathing:** Inhale.
**Mind:** Imagine Chi going from both sides of the sky into both palms.

**Movement 2:** Push both arms out until your elbows are straight again. (See photo 78.)
**Breathing:** Exhale.
**Mind:** Imagine Chi going out from both palms.

## (39) Get Chi from the Left and Right Sides of the Sky 6

*Zuo You De Qi 6*

**Movement 1:** Keeping both hands pointing out to the sides, pull them toward your shoulder until the elbows are at a 90-degree angle. (See photo 79.)
**Breathing:** Inhale.
**Mind:** Imagine Chi going from both sides of the sky into both palms.

**Movement 2:** Push both arms out until your elbows are straight again. (See photo 80.)
**Breathing:** Exhale.
**Mind:** Imagine Chi going out from both palms.

## (40) Get Chi from the Outer Left and Right Front Sides of the Sky 1

*Zuo You Qian Yai Feng De Qi 1*

**Movement 1:** Keeping your fingers pointing up and elbows straight, bring your arms to the front of your body until your hands are at 45 degrees to your body. (See photo 81.)

**Breathing:** Inhale.

**Mind:** Imagine Chi going from the left and right front sides of the sky into both palms.

**Movement 2:** Bring your arms back until they are aligned with your shoulders. (See photo 82.)

**Breathing:** Exhale.

**Mind:** Imagine Chi going out from both palms.

# (41) Get Chi from the Outer Left and Right Front Sides of the Sky 2

## *Zuo You Qian Yai Feng De Qi 2*

**Movement 1:** Keeping your fingers pointing up and elbows straight, bring your arms to the front of your body until your hands are at 45 degrees to your body. (See photo 83.)

**Breathing:** Inhale.

**Mind:** Imagine Chi going from the left and right front sides of the sky into both palms.

**Movement 2:** Bring your arms back until they are aligned with your shoulders. (See photo 84.)

**Breathing:** Exhale.

**Mind:** Imagine Chi going out from both palms.

## (42) Get Chi from the Outer Left and Right Front Sides of the Sky 3

*Zuo You Qian Yai Feng De Qi 3*

**Movement 1:** Keeping your fingers pointing up and elbows straight, bring your arms to the front of your body until your hands are at 45 degrees to your body. (See photo 85.)
**Breathing:** Inhale.
**Mind:** Imagine Chi going from the left and right front sides of the sky into both palms.

**Movement 2:** Bring your arms back until they are aligned with your shoulders. (See photo 86.)
**Breathing:** Exhale.
**Mind:** Imagine Chi going out from both palms.

# (43) Two Hands Moving Toward Each Other

*Shuan Shou Kao Long*

**Movement 1:** Bring both your arms back to the front of the body until they are a shoulder-width apart. Keep your fingers and palms up. (See photo 87.)

**Breathing:** Inhale.

**Mind:** Imagine Chi going from outside into both palms.

87

**Movement 2:** Push both palms forward with a slight tension. (See photo 88.)

**Breathing:** Exhale.

**Mind:** Imagine Chi going out from both palms.

88

## (44) Get Chi from the Front Side of the Sky 4

*Zheng Qian Mian De Qi 4*

**Movement 1:** Keeping palms up, pull both hands back until your elbows are bending at 90 degrees. (See photo 89.)

**Breathing:** Inhale.

**Mind:** Imagine Chi going from the front edge of the sky into both palms.

**Movement 2:** Push your hands forward slightly until your elbows are straight again. (See photo 90.)

**Breathing:** Exhale.

**Mind:** Imagine both palms reaching the front edge of the sky and Chi going out from them.

# (45) Get Chi from the Front Side of the Sky 5

## *Zheng Qian Mian De Qi 5*

**Movement 1:** Keeping palms up, pull both hands back until your elbows are bending at 90 degrees. (See photo 91.)

**Breathing:** Inhale.

**Mind:** Imagine Chi going from the front edge of the sky into both palms.

**Movement 2:** Push your hands forward slightly until your elbows are straight again. (See photo 92.)

**Breathing:** Exhale.

**Mind:** Imagine both palms reaching the front edge of the sky and Chi going out from them.

## (46) Get Chi from the Front Side of the Sky 6

*Zheng Qian Mian De Qi 6*

**Movement 1:** Keeping your palms up, pull both hands back until your elbows are bending at 90 degrees. (See photo 93.)

**Breathing:** Inhale.

**Mind:** Imagine Chi going from the front edge of the sky into both palms.

**Movement 2:** Push your hands forward slightly until your elbows are straight again. (See photo 94.)

**Breathing:** Exhale.

**Mind:** Imagine both palms reaching the front edge of sky and Chi going out from them.

# (47) Get Chi from the Upper Front Sides of the Sky 1

*Qian Shang Feng De Qi 1*

**Movement 1:** Keeping your palms and fingers up, move your hands up 45 degrees from shoulder level. (See photo 95.)
**Breathing:** Inhale.
**Mind:** Imagine Chi going from the upper front sides of the sky into both palms.

**Movement 2:** Move both hands downward until they are at shoulder level again. (See photo 96.)
**Breathing:** Exhale.
**Mind:** Imagine Chi going out from both palms.

## (48) Get Chi from the Upper Front Sides of the Sky 2

*Qiang Shang Feng De Qi 2*

**Movement 1:** Keeping your palms and fingers up, move your hands up 45 degrees from shoulder level again. (See photo 97.)
**Breathing:** Inhale.
**Mind:** Imagine Chi going from the upper front sides of the sky into both palms.

**Movement 2:** Move both hands downward until they are at shoulder level again. (See photo 98.)
**Breathing:** Exhale.
**Mind:** Imagine Chi going out from both palms.

## (49) Get Chi from the Upper Front Sides of the Sky 3

*Qian Shang Feng De Qi 3*

**Movement 1:** Keeping your palms and fingers up, move your hands up 45 degrees from shoulder level again. (See photo 99.)
**Breathing:** Inhale.
**Mind:** Imagine Chi going from the upper front sides of the sky into both palms.

**Movement 2:** Move both hands downward until they are at shoulder level again. (See photo 100.)
**Breathing:** Exhale.
**Mind:** Imagine Chi going out from both palms.

## (50) Direct Chi to Baihui

*Ying Qi Dao Baihui*

**Movement 1:** Turn your palms up. Raise your arms over your head so that your palms now face down. (See photos 101 and 102.)
**Breathing:** Inhale.
**Mind:** Imagine Chi being held in both palms.

**Movement 2:** Press both palms with a slight tension toward your Baihui. Hold for 2 to 3 seconds. (See photo 103.)
**Breathing:** Exhale.
**Mind:** Imagine Chi going from both palms into your Baihui.

101

103

102

## (51) Direct Chi to Yintang

### *Ying Qi Dao Yintang*

**Movement 1:** Move the palms of your hands down over your face until they reach the level of your Yintang. (See photo 104.)

**Breathing:** Inhale.

**Mind:** Imagine Chi going between both palms to your head and face.

104

**Movement 2:** Press your middle fingers gently on your Yintang. (See photo 105.)

**Breathing:** Exhale.

**Mind:** Imagine Chi going from both middle fingers into your Yintang.

105

## (52) Direct Chi to Fengfu

*Ying Qi Dao Fengfu*

106

**Movement 1:** Move your hands back until your two middle fingers touch each other behind your head. Now press both middle fingers gently on your Fengfu. (See photos 106 and 107.)
**Breathing:** Inhale.
**Mind:** Imagine Chi going between your palms and head.

**Movement 2:** Press your middle fingers gently on your Fengfu. (See photo 108.)
**Breathing:** Exhale.
**Mind:** Imagine Chi going from both middle fingers into your Fengfu.

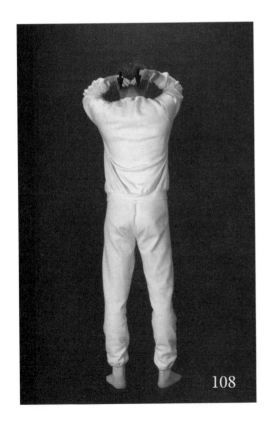

108

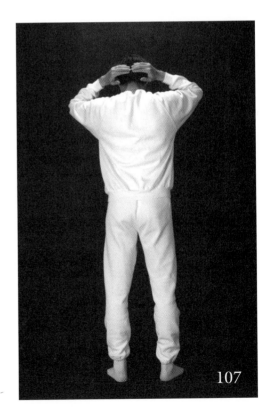

107

## (53) Direct Chi to Dazhui 1

*Ying Qi Dao Dazhui 1*

**Movement 1:** Move both hands down your back until both middle fingers reach the level of your Dazhui.
**Breathing:** Inhale.
**Mind:** Imagine Chi going between both palms and your back.

**Movement 2:** Press your middle fingers gently on your Dazhui. (See photo 109.)
**Breathing:** Exhale.
**Mind:** Imagine Chi going from both middle fingers into your Dazhui.

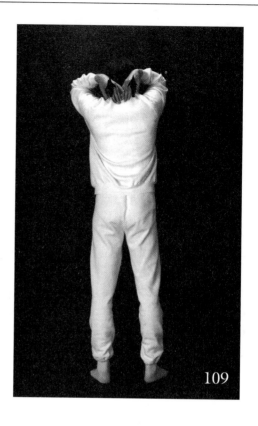

109

## (54) Direct Chi to Dazhui 2

### *Ying Qi Dao Dazhui 2*

**Movement 1:** Move your hands upward first to reach your shoulders, then forward and downward to reach your chest, then back down under your arms until both middle fingers reach your Dazhui. If your middle fingers cannot reach your Dazhui, then just imagine they reach it. (See photos 110 and 111.)

**Breathing:** Inhale.

**Mind:** Imagine Chi going between both palms and your shoulder, chest, and back.

**Movement 2:** Press both middle fingers gently on your Dazhui. (See photo 112.)

**Breathing:** Exhale.

**Mind:** Imagine Chi going from both middle fingers into your Dazhui.

110

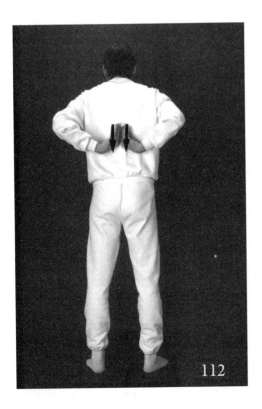

112

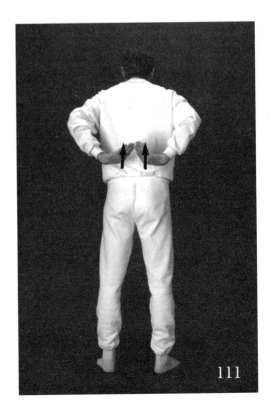

111

## (55) Direct Chi to Mingmen

*Ying Qi Dao Mingmen*

**Movement 1:** Move both hands downward along your back until you reach the level of your Mingmen. (See photo 113.)
**Breathing:** Inhale.
**Mind:** Imagine Chi going between both palms and your back.

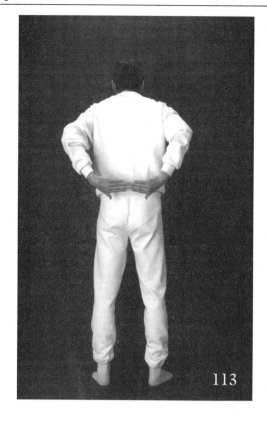

**Movement 2:** Press both middle fingers gently on your Mingmen. (See photo 114.)
**Breathing:** Exhale.
**Mind:** Imagine Chi going from both middle fingers into your Mingmen.

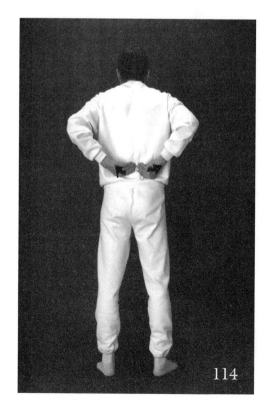

# FIFTH SEQUENCE
## (56–63)

## (56) Direct Chi to Dantian

*Ying Qi Dao Dantian*

**Movement 1:** Place your palms flatly on both sides of your lower back, then move them forward until both reach the front of your abdomen at the level of your Dantian. (See photos 115 and 116.)

**Breathing:** Inhale.

**Mind:** Imagine Chi going between both palms and both sides of your back and abdomen.

**Movement 2:** Use both middle fingers to press gently on your Dantian. (See photo 117.)

**Breathing:** Exhale.

**Mind:** Imagine Chi going into your Dantian from both middle fingers.

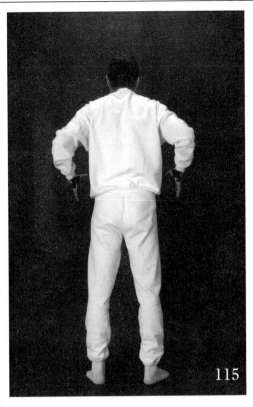

115

117

116

## (57) Direct Chi to Yongquan

*Ying Qi Dao Yongquan*

**Movement 1:** Bend slowly forward, keeping your legs and knees straight while your arms are hanging down. Slide both palms down the front of your thighs along your legs to the top of your feet. As you slide the palms down, bend your knees as needed. Stop when you reach your toes. (See photo 118.)

**Breathing:** Inhale.

**Mind:** Imagine Chi going between both palms and the front side of your thighs, legs, top of your feet, and toes.

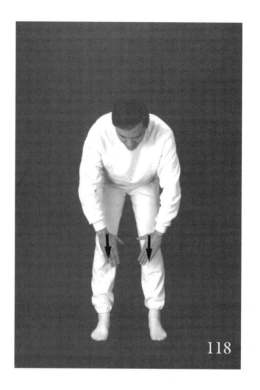

118

**Movement 2:** Press both palms over your toes. (See photo 119.)

**Breathing:** Exhale.

**Mind:** Imagine Chi going from both palms to your Yongquan.

119

## (58) Connect Chi Between Dantian and Yongquan 4

*Lian Jie Dantian Yongquan 4*

**Movement 1:** Lift your hands up off your toes as you bring up your body and straighten your knees. Stop when your hands reach the level of your knees. (See photo 120.)

**Breathing:** Inhale.

**Mind:** Imagine Chi coming from the earth to the Yongquan and then through both feet, legs, and thighs to your Dantian.

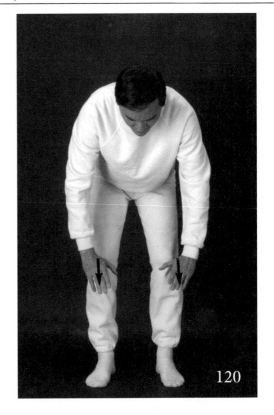

**Movement 2:** Move your body back down and bend your knees until both palms are pressing your toes. (See photo 121.)

**Breathing:** Exhale.

**Mind:** Imagine Chi coming from the Dantian through the thighs, legs, feet, and then going out from the Yongquan to the earth.

## (59) Connect Chi Between Dantian and Yongquan 5

*Lian Jie Dantian Yongquan 5*

**Movement 1:** Lift your hands up off your toes as you bring up your body and straighten your knees. Stop when your hands reach the level of your knees. (See photo 122.)

**Breathing:** Inhale.

**Mind:** Imagine Chi coming from the earth to the Yongquan, then through both feet, legs, and thighs to your Dantian.

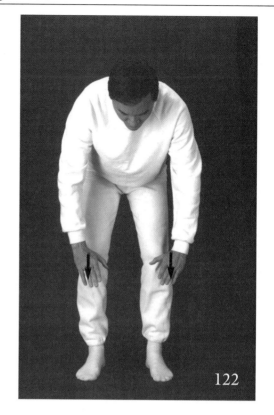

122

**Movement 2:** Move your body back down and bend your knees until both palms are pressing your toes. (See photo 123.)

**Breathing:** Exhale.

**Mind:** Imagine Chi coming from the Dantian through the thighs, legs, feet, and then going out from the Yongquan to the earth.

123

## (60) Connect Chi Between Dantian and Yongquan 6

*Lian Jie Dantian Yongquan 6*

**Movement 1:** Lift your hands up off your toes as you bring up your body and straighten your knees. Stop when your hands reach the level of your knees. (See photo 124.)

**Breathing:** Inhale.

**Mind:** Imagine Chi coming from the earth to the Yongquan, then through both feet, legs, and thighs to the Dantian.

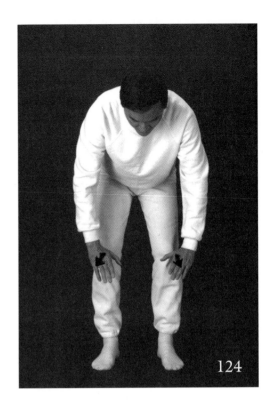

**Movement 2:** Move the body downward and bend the knees; press both palms on the toes of both feet. (See photo 123).

**Breathing:** Exhale.

**Mind:** Imagine Chi coming from the Dantian through the thighs, legs, feet, and then going out from the Yongquan to the earth.

## (61) Direct Chi to Mingmen

*Ying Qi Dao Mingmen*

**Movement 1:** As you bring your body back upward, slide your palms over the top of your feet, then the back of your legs, and up your thighs and buttocks. As you slide them up, straighten your knees and waist. Stop when your reach your Mingmen. (See photos 125 and 126.)

**Breathing:** Inhale.

**Mind:** Imagine Chi coming from the Yongquan and then going between both palms and the top of your feet, back of legs, thighs, buttocks, and Mingmen.

**Movement 2:** Press both middle fingers gently on your Mingmen. (See photo 127.)

**Breathing:** Exhale.

**Mind:** Imagine Chi going from both middle fingers into the Mingmen.

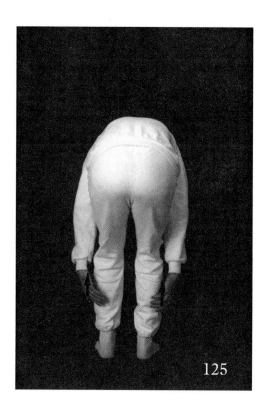

125

127

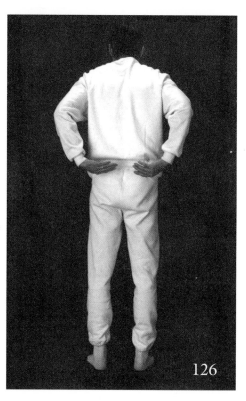

126

79

## (62) Direct Chi to Dantian

*Ying Qi Dao Dantian*

**Movement 1:** Place your palms flat on both sides of your lower back, then move them forward until both reach the front of your abdomen at the level of your Dantian. (See photos 128 and 129.)

**Breathing:** Inhale.

**Mind:** Imagine Chi going between both palms and both sides of your back and abdomen.

**Movement 2:** Press both middle fingers gently into your Dantian. (See photo 130.)

**Breathing:** Exhale.

**Mind:** Imagine Chi going from both middle fingers into the Dantian.

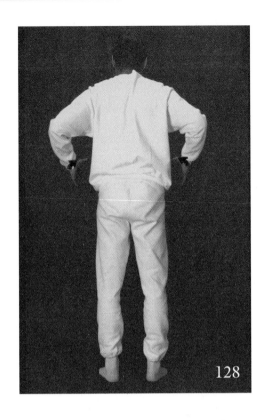

128

130

129

## (63) Bring Chi Back to the Earth

*Qi Qui Di Qiu*

**Movement 1:** Separate your hands and move them slowly downward and outward from your Dantian. Let your arms hang naturally at the sides of your body.
**Breathing:** Inhale.
**Mind:** Imagine Chi going from your Dantian to both palms.

**Movement 2:** With both palms facing downward and fingers pointing forward, press both palms downward slightly. (See photo 131.)
**Breathing:** Exhale.
**Mind:** Imagine Chi going from both palms back to the earth.

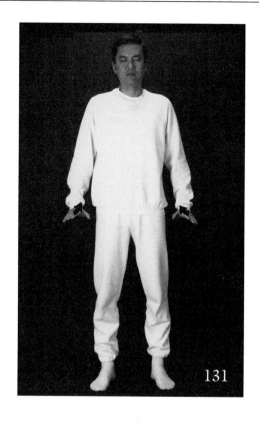

131

# SIXTH SEQUENCE
## (64–75)

## (64) Direct Chi to Baihui

*Ying Qi Dao Baihui*

**Movement 1:** Turn both palms to face inward and lift them up in front of your abdomen, chest, and face until they are above your head. (See photos 132 and 133.)

**Breathing:** Inhale.

**Mind:** Imagine Chi being held between your two palms.

**Movement 2:** Turn both palms to face your Baihui, then press them toward your Baihui with a slight tension. Hold for 2 to 3 seconds. (See photo 134.)

**Breathing:** Exhale.

**Mind:** Imagine Chi going in from both palms.

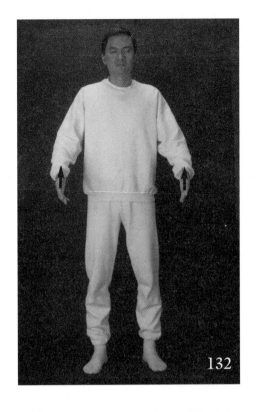

132

134

133

## (65) Push Chi Out with the Right Palm

*Yao Zhang Tui Qi*

**Movement 1:** Move both hands down to the level of your chest. Turn your palms up and facing forward. Point your fingers upward. (See photo 135.)

**Breathing:** Inhale.

**Mind:** Imagine Chi being held in both palms.

**Movement 2:** Push your right hand forward until your right elbow is only slightly bent. (See photo 136.)

**Breathing:** Exhale.

**Mind:** Imagine Chi going out from the right palm and being pushed forward.

## (66) Direct Chi to the Left Qihu

*Ying Qi Dao Zuo Qihu*

**Movement 1:** Move your right hand over to the left side of your body until it reaches the heart region of your body. As you move your right hand, let your torso turn as well for about 45 degrees. (See photo 137.)

**Breathing:** Inhale.

**Mind:** Imagine Chi being held in the right palm.

137

**Movement 2:** Press the middle finger of your right hand gently on the left Qihu. (See photo 138.)

**Breathing:** Exhale.

**Mind:** Imagine Chi going from the right middle finger into the left Qihu.

138

## (67) Push Chi Out with the Left Palm

*Zuo Zhang Tui Qi*

**Movement 1:** Turn your torso facing forward again. Your left palm is facing forward and your fingers are pointing up. Your right hand remains on your left Qihu. (See photo 139.)

**Breathing:** Inhale.

**Mind:** Imagine Chi being held in the left palm.

139

**Movement 2:** Push your left hand forward until your left elbow is slightly bent. (See photo 140.)

**Breathing:** Exhale.

**Mind:** Imagine Chi going out from the left palm and being pushed forward.

140

## (68) Direct Chi to the Right Qihu

*Ying Qi Dao You Qihu*

**Movement 1:** Move your left hand over to the right side of your body until it reaches the heart region of your body. As you move your left hand, let your torso turn as well for about 45 degrees. (See photo 141.)

**Breathing:** Inhale.

**Mind:** Imagine Chi being held in the left palm.

**Movement 2:** Press the middle finger of your left hand gently on your right Qihu. At this time, your two wrists are crossing each other with your left wrist on the outside. (See photo 142.)

**Breathing:** Exhale.

**Mind:** Imagine Chi going from the left middle finger into the right Qihu.

# (69) Press Palms in Front of the Chest

*Xiong Qian He Zhang*

**Movement 1:** Move both hands a little forward and uncurl your wrists so that now their insides touch each other. Your hands should form a cup. (See photo 143.)
**Breathing:** Inhale.
**Mind:** Imagine Chi being held within both palms.

143

**Movement 2:** Press your palms lightly into each other in front of your chest. Your fingers should be pointing up and the tip of your thumbs pointing at your chest. (See photo 144.)
**Breathing:** Exhale.
**Mind:** Imagine Chi going out from your fingers and thumbs to the sky.

144

## (70) Get Chi from the Upper Sky

*Shang Feng De Qi*

**Movement 1:** Keep your palms pressed together and stretch them slowly upward over your head until your shoulders and elbows are extended. (See photo 145.)

**Breathing:** Inhale.

**Mind:** Imagine the two palms reaching the sky and Chi coming from the sky into both of them.

**Movement 2:** Turn both palms facing forward. Keep your fingers together and let the tip of your thumbs and index and middle fingers touch to form a triangle. (See photo 146.)

**Breathing:** Exhale.

**Mind:** Imagine Chi going out from the triangle formed between your thumbs and index fingers.

# (71) Separate Hands

*Liang Shou Feng Kai*

**Movement 1:** Keeping your palms facing forward, lower your hands to the sides of your body until your two hands are at shoulder level. (See photo 147.)

**Breathing:** Inhale.

**Mind:** Imagine Chi going from the left and right sides of the edge of the sky into both palms.

147

**Movement 2:** Turn both palms facing up. (See photo 148.)

**Breathing:** Exhale.

**Mind:** Imagine Chi going out from both palms.

148

## (72) Direct Chi to Yintang

*Ying Qi Dao Yintang*

**Movement 1:** Turn both palms upward; bring both hands forward until they are a shoulder-width apart. Then bring your palms so that they face your face. (See photo 149.)

**Breathing:** Inhale.

**Mind:** Imagine Chi going from the outside into both palms.

**Movement 2:** With your fingers pointing upward, press both palms lightly against your Yintang. Hold for 2 to 3 seconds. (See photo 150.)

**Breathing:** Exhale.

**Mind:** Imagine Chi going from both palms into the Yintang.

# (73) Direct Chi to Dabao

*Ying Qi Dao Dabao*

**Movement 1:** Move both hands back until they are under your armpits. Your palms are facing up and your fingers are pointing toward your body. (See photo 151.)
**Breathing:** Inhale.
**Mind:** Imagine Chi being held in both palms.

**Movement 2:** Press both middle fingers gently toward your Dabao. (See photo 152.)
**Breathing:** Exhale.
**Mind:** Imagine Chi going from your palms through the middle fingers into your Dabao.

## (74) Circulate Chi to Dantian

*Lan Qi Dao Dantian*

**Movement 1:** Continue moving both hands back to your back, then forward to the sides of your body, then to the front of your body, and finally back to your Dantian. (See photos 153 and 154.)
**Breathing:** Inhale.
**Mind:** Imagine Chi going from outside into both palms.

*continued on next page*

153

154

**Movement 2:** Press both palms gently on your Dantian and hold for 2 to 3 seconds. For men, your left palm touches your Dantian while your right palm covers the left palm. For women, your right palm touches your Dantian and your left palm covers the right palm. Based on traditional Chinese medicine, Chi goes out better from the right palm (to the Dantian) than the left, for women. The opposite is true for men. (See photo 155.)

**Breathing:** Exhale.

**Mind:** Imagine Chi going from both palms into your Dantian.

155

## (75) Closing

*Shou Shi*

**Movement 1:** Separate your hands and push both palms slightly downward with your fingers pointing forward. (See photo 156.)
**Breathing:** Inhale.
**Mind:** Imagine Chi going from the Dantian to both palms.

156

**Movement 2:** Continue moving your hands downward and outward to the sides of your body. Let your arms hang naturally and your fingers point down. (See photo 157.)
**Breathing:** Exhale.
**Mind:** Imagine Chi going from both palms back to the earth.

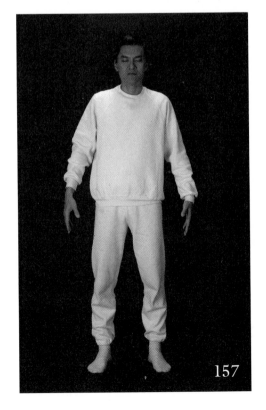

157

# INDEX

# ABOUT THE AUTHORS

Wei Yue Sun, M.D., graduated with his medical degree in 1988 from the Sun Yat-sen University of Medical Sciences in Guangzhou, People's Republic of China. He currently is a public health epidemiologist in the New York City Department of Health. He has practiced both traditional Chinese medicine and Western medicine in China. Dr. Sun has practiced and taught different styles of Chi Kung and Tai Chi Chuan for many years in both China and the United States.

Xiao Jing Li, M.D., graduated from Guangzhou Medical College in Guangzhou, People's Republic of China, in 1986. She is a research associate in molecular biology at City University of New York. She has practiced and taught Chi Kung and Tai Chi Chuan for years. She has also practiced acupuncture and Chinese herbology for years in China. Dr. Li has been practicing both traditional Chinese medicine and Western medicine for more than 10 years. She has developed new therapies by combining ancient Chinese medical theories and modern Western medical techniques. She is currently a U.S. NCCA Board Certified medical doctor. Dr. Li will soon open an acupuncture, Chinese herbology medicine, and natural healing center.

Dr. Sun and Dr. Li have done research in the areas of Chi Kung and health. The Chi Kung techniques presented in this book are the result of years of practice and scientific research by Dr. Sun and Dr. Li.